AN ENTREPRENEUR WHO HASN'T FAILED YET!

THE STORY OF TRYING, FAILING AND NOT GIVING UP.

MAYANK BANSAL

This book is dedicated to all young entrepreneurs who dare to dream and strive to make a positive impact in the world. Your passion, creativity, and determination are the seeds of change that can inspire generations to come. May your journey be filled with courage, resilience, and the unwavering belief that you can do something good in life. Keep pushing boundaries and believing in yourself—you are the future!

Contents

Preface

In this book, you'll discover the critical reasons behind business failures, often stemming from poor decision-making and a lack of industry knowledge. Simply jumping into an investment without proper understanding rarely leads to success.

Over the past few years, I've invested my time, money, and resources in various businesses—from the hotel industry to stock brokering—but many of these ventures did not yield the success I had hoped for. However, every setback taught me invaluable lessons.

I've come to realise that several factors contributed to these failures, such as entering industries outside my expertise, starting ventures without adequate experience, or getting swept away by excitement over new opportunities while neglecting existing commitments.

Determined to learn from my past, I've worked diligently to approach new ventures with careful consideration and informed decision-making. This book encapsulates my journey, offering insights and strategies that can help young entrepreneurs navigate the complexities of starting or revitalising a business.

By engaging with the chapters ahead, you'll find practical guidance designed to simplify your decision-making process. My goal is to present these concepts in an accessible manner, so you can easily grasp and apply them to your entrepreneurial endeavours.

Acknowledgements

I would like to express my heartfelt gratitude to my parents, whose unwavering support and belief in me have been the foundation of my journey. Your love and guidance have shaped me into the person I am today, and I am forever grateful for your encouragement.

To my sister Mamta, thank you for always being my confidante and cheerleader. Your insights and laughter have brightened even the toughest days. To my brother-in-law Hemant, I appreciate your wise counsel and the way you've embraced my dreams as your own.

A special thank you to my brother Sandeep and sister-in-law Ketki. Your encouragement and support means a lot to me, and I am grateful to have you both by my side.

And to Nikita, your support and encouragement have been invaluable throughout this process. I truly appreciate your willingness to listen and offer insights that have helped me grow.

This book reflects not only my journey but also the incredible people who have walked alongside me. Thank you all for believing in me.

'FALLING FORWARD'

TURNING LOSSES INTO STEPPING STONES FOR SUCCESS

Redefining Failure

In my experience, failure isn't the end—it's an opportunity to learn. I believe that redefining failure is crucial for any entrepreneur. Instead of seeing failure as something negative, view it as a valuable experience. Each setback provides insights into what went wrong and how you can improve in the future.

Understanding that failure is a natural part of the journey toward success can change your perspective. Everyone faces obstacles; it's how we respond to them that matters. For me, every failed business taught me lessons that helped shape my future decisions. These lessons often revealed what to avoid and how to approach problems differently.

The long-term benefits of falling forward are significant. Each time you stumble, you gather knowledge that contributes to your growth. Instead of feeling discouraged, use those experiences to fuel your determination. I've encountered many failures, but I've always tried to extract lessons from them. This mindset has allowed me to build stronger businesses over time.

When you embrace failure as part of your journey, you open yourself up to new possibilities. It helps you become more resilient and adaptable, qualities that are essential for success. Remember, every setback can be a stepping stone if you choose to learn from it. By shifting your mindset, you can turn losses into valuable lessons that pave the way for your future success.

The Mindset Shift: From Setback to Comeback

One of the most important lessons I've learned as an entrepreneur is how to shift my mindset from viewing setbacks as failures to seeing them as opportunities for growth. Whenever I face a challenge, I remind myself that each obstacle can teach me something valuable. Instead of dwelling on past mistakes, I keep my mind open to new potential ventures and ideas.

Creating a personal success narrative is also crucial. By writing my story to highlight how I've grown from my failures, I can better understand my journey. This is part of why I'm writing this book—to share my experiences and show that setbacks can lead to greater success.

Celebrating small victories along the way is another key strategy I use. Each time I achieve a little goal, I take a moment to recognize that progress. These small wins help lift me out of any mental stress caused by past failures. They remind me that I'm moving forward, one step at a time.

By focusing on these small victories, I build my confidence and motivation. This positive reinforcement helps me stay resilient and encourages me to keep pushing toward my larger goals. Remember, it's not just about the big wins; it's the small achievements that pave the way for your ultimate success. Embrace the journey, learn from your experiences, and celebrate every step forward.

Lessons Learned: Analyzing Your Losses

One of the most important steps in turning losses into successes is analyzing what went wrong. After a setback, I always take the time to reflect on the reasons behind my failure. I often ask myself questions repeatedly: What could I have done differently? What lessons can I learn? This self-reflection helps me find answers and allows me to avoid making the same mistakes in the future.

Sharing these lessons with others is another way to turn my experiences into something positive. By telling my story, I hope to inspire and help other entrepreneurs facing similar challenges. When you share your journey, you not only help others but also reinforce your own learning.

Positive self-talk plays a significant role in recovery and growth. The way we talk to ourselves can influence our mindset. When I face difficulties, I try to replace negative thoughts with encouraging ones. Instead of saying, "I failed," I remind myself, "I'm learning and getting better." This shift in internal dialogue can make a big difference in how we recover from setbacks.

In summary, analyzing your losses, sharing what you've learned, and practising positive self-talk can transform your failures into stepping stones for success. Every setback is a chance to grow and improve, leading you closer to your goals. Embrace these experiences and use them to fuel your journey forward.

Overcoming Fear of Failure

Overcoming the fear of failure is essential for any entrepreneur. When faced with uncertainty, it's easy to let fear hold you back. One strategy I use is to break down my fears into smaller parts. Instead of thinking, "What if I fail?" I ask myself, "What can I learn from this?" This shift in thinking helps me manage my fear and see challenges as opportunities for growth.

Another important aspect of my journey has been learning to turn criticism into growth. Feedback, whether positive or negative, can be incredibly valuable. When someone offers criticism, I try not to take it personally. Instead, I view it as a chance to improve. I ask myself, "How can I use this feedback to become better?" This mindset helps me develop both personally and professionally.

For example, if a project doesn't go as planned, I gather feedback from my team or clients. Their insights can reveal areas I may not have noticed. By embracing criticism and learning from it, I can make necessary adjustments for the future.

In conclusion, overcoming the fear of failure and turning criticism into growth are powerful tools for any entrepreneur. By changing the way you view challenges and feedback, you can transform setbacks into valuable lessons that pave the way for your success. Remember, every experience is an opportunity to learn and grow.

Setting New Goals After a Loss

After experiencing a loss, setting new goals is crucial. It's easy to feel discouraged, but redefining your objectives can help you stay motivated. I always take a moment to reflect on what went wrong and what I can learn from it. Then, I set new, achievable goals that are aligned with my growth. For example, if a project didn't succeed, instead of focusing on that failure, I ask myself, "What do I want to achieve next?" This shift in focus helps me move forward with renewed energy.

Transforming losses into opportunities is another vital skill. Every setback holds potential if you know where to look. When something doesn't go as planned, I try to identify what new paths might be opening up. For instance, if a business idea flops, I might discover a gap in the market that I hadn't considered before. By staying curious and open-minded, I can often turn a negative situation into a new venture.

Techniques for spotting opportunities include brainstorming sessions and seeking feedback from others. I find that talking to my team or mentors can spark ideas I hadn't thought of.

In summary, setting new goals and transforming losses into opportunities are powerful ways to keep moving forward. Embrace setbacks as stepping stones toward your next success, and remember that every challenge can lead to new possibilities if you keep your mind open.

Creating an Action Plan

Creating an action plan is essential when moving forward after a setback. After experiencing failure, I realized that having a clear plan helps me regain focus and motivation. The first step is to analyze what went wrong and what I can learn from it. Once I understand the lessons, I outline specific actions I can take. This might include setting new goals, seeking advice, or adjusting my strategies.

It's also important to have a Plan B. In my experience, relying solely on one approach can lead to disappointment. If Plan A doesn't work, I can quickly switch to Plan B, which keeps me moving forward. This flexibility has saved me from feeling stuck after failures.

Persistence plays a crucial role in turning setbacks into successes. Tenacity is about keeping going, even when things get tough. There were times when I faced challenges that seemed insurmountable. However, by staying committed and pushing through, I eventually found breakthroughs that led to success. Each time I faced a hurdle, I reminded myself that persistence often pays off.

In summary, creating an action plan and being persistent are vital for bouncing back from losses. Embrace your setbacks as opportunities to learn and grow. With a clear plan and a tenacious spirit, you can turn failures into stepping stones on your path to success. Remember, every setback is just a setup for a comeback!

The Importance of Support Systems

Having a strong support system is crucial when facing setbacks. In my journey, I've encountered people who only think about themselves and even try to bring me down. It's frustrating to be around those who find joy in others' failures instead of focusing on their own paths. But I've learned to seek out a different circle—one filled with people who uplift and encourage me. Surrounding myself with supportive individuals has made a significant difference in my mindset.

My parents have always been my biggest supporters. They believe in me even when I doubt myself. Their encouragement reminds me that I'm not alone in my journey. Building a network of positive influences has helped me stay resilient and motivated, especially during tough times.

Another helpful practice I've adopted is mindfulness. When faced with challenges, mindfulness allows me to pause and reflect rather than react impulsively. It helps me stay calm and focused, enabling me to navigate obstacles more effectively. Taking a moment to breathe and assess the situation can turn a stressful moment into an opportunity for growth.

In summary, creating a strong support system and practising mindfulness can help you turn losses into stepping stones to success. Surround yourself with those who encourage you, and use mindfulness to manage adversity. With the right mindset and support, you can transform setbacks into valuable lessons on your path to success.

"Failure isn't the end; it's a chance to learn. Each setback offers insights that lead to future success."

CHAPTER TWO

'NUMBERS SPEAK LOUDER'

THE CLARITY BEYOND WORDS

The Power of Data in Decision-Making

I've come to recognize the immense power of data in decision-making. Early on, I struggled to communicate my ideas effectively because I lacked the concrete data to back them up. This experience taught me a crucial lesson: numbers speak louder than words. When you present your ideas with solid data, you significantly increase their impact and credibility.

Data-driven decision-making allows you to make strategic choices based on factual insights rather than intuition alone. For instance, analytics plays a critical role in understanding customer behaviour. By examining trends and preferences through data, you can refine customer experiences, tailoring your products and services to meet their needs. This not only enhances customer satisfaction but also drives loyalty and repeat business.

Additionally, market research numbers are vital for shaping your understanding of the competitive landscape. Statistics provide insights into market size, demographics, and emerging trends, enabling you to identify opportunities and potential pitfalls. With accurate data, you can make informed decisions about product development, pricing strategies, and marketing efforts.

In conclusion, harnessing the power of data is essential for effective decision-making. By integrating analytics into your strategy, you enhance your ability to articulate ideas, understand customer needs, and navigate the market landscape. Embrace the numbers, and you'll find that they empower you to make more confident and informed choices on your entrepreneurial journey.

The Cost of Ignoring Data

I've learned the hard way about the cost of ignoring data. Early on, I frequently made decisions without the necessary metrics, resulting in low outcomes and unrealized profits. My lack of data management led to missed opportunities and misguided strategies, ultimately affecting the sustainability of my ventures.

Maintaining a proper ledger and tracking your sales and expenses is crucial for any business. When you don't have accurate data, you risk making uninformed decisions that can steer your business off course. For instance, without clear insights into your financials, it's challenging to identify which products are performing well and which ones are not. This lack of visibility can lead to overspending in areas that do not yield a return on investment.

My experiences with financial loss across various ventures taught me that data is not just a technicality; it's a necessity. Each setback reinforced the importance of diligent record-keeping and regular analysis. By prioritizing data management, you gain the ability to make informed decisions based on real-time insights rather than guesswork.

In conclusion, please don't ignore the data. Embrace it as a valuable tool that guides your business strategies and enhances your decision-making process. By leveraging metrics effectively, you empower yourself to navigate challenges more adeptly and unlock your business's full potential. Remember, informed choices lead to sustainable success.

Using Numbers to Evaluate Marketing ROI

I've learned that effectively using numbers is crucial for evaluating marketing ROI. Understanding the effectiveness of your marketing efforts is essential for optimizing your strategies and ensuring that every dollar spent delivers value. By analyzing metrics such as conversion rates, customer acquisition costs, and overall sales, you can assess what works and what doesn't.

Data-driven innovation is another key aspect of leveraging numbers. Insights derived from data can inform product development and guide you in creating solutions that meet real customer needs. For instance, by examining customer feedback and market trends, you can identify gaps in the market and innovate accordingly, ensuring your offerings resonate with your target audience.

Translating raw data into meaningful insights is a vital skill for any entrepreneur. Techniques such as data visualization and statistical analysis can help you interpret complex information in a way that reveals patterns and trends. This not only aids in decision-making but also enhances your ability to communicate findings to stakeholders.

Finally, storytelling with numbers can elevate your data presentation. Crafting narratives around data-driven insights allows you to convey the significance of your findings compellingly. This approach not only captures attention but also helps others understand the broader implications of the data.

In conclusion, harnessing the power of numbers is essential for evaluating marketing effectiveness, driving innovation, and making informed decisions. By transforming raw data into actionable insights and compelling stories, you can significantly enhance your entrepreneurial success.

The Psychology of Numbers

Understanding the psychology of numbers is essential for

any entrepreneur. Numerical data significantly influences behavior and perception, shaping how we make decisions and assess success. People tend to respond more favorably to quantifiable information, which can enhance your ability to persuade and motivate others. By presenting data effectively, you can guide stakeholders and customers toward desired actions.

Data visualization plays a critical role in making sense of numbers. Effective charts and graphs can transform complex data sets into easily digestible information, allowing you to communicate insights clearly and persuasively. Visual tools not only capture attention but also help audiences grasp trends and patterns quickly, facilitating informed decision-making.

Additionally, setting SMART goals—Specific, Measurable, Achievable, Relevant, and Time-bound—is integral to your success. Metrics serve as the backbone of this framework, providing a clear structure for evaluating progress. By defining your goals with precise metrics, you create a roadmap that guides your actions and decisions. This approach allows you to measure success objectively, making adjustments as needed to stay on track.

In summary, the power of numbers extends beyond mere data; it shapes perceptions, drives behavior, and informs strategic decisions. By harnessing effective data visualization techniques and employing metrics to set SMART goals, you empower yourself and your team to achieve meaningful results. Embrace the psychology of numbers to enhance your entrepreneurial journey and foster a culture of accountability and growth.

Benchmarking Against the Competition

In today's competitive landscape, benchmarking against the competition is vital for understanding your market positioning and performance. By analyzing industry data, you can identify your strengths and weaknesses relative to competitors. This process not only highlights areas for improvement but also helps you capitalize on your unique advantages.

Incorporating feedback loops into your strategy enables continuous improvement. By systematically collecting and analyzing data, you can refine processes and products iteratively. This approach fosters a culture of growth, encouraging teams to learn from past experiences and make data-informed adjustments that drive better outcomes.

Measuring customer sentiment through data is another powerful technique for enhancing your business. Tools like surveys, social media analytics, and customer reviews provide valuable insights into how your audience perceives your brand. By quantifying and interpreting this feedback, you can tailor your offerings to meet customer needs more effectively, boosting satisfaction and loyalty.

Real-world case studies abound of businesses that thrived through data-driven decisions. Companies like Netflix and Amazon leverage data to personalize customer experiences and optimize operations, setting industry standards. These success stories illustrate how a commitment to using data can lead to substantial growth and innovation.

In conclusion, harnessing the power of data—through benchmarking, feedback loops, customer sentiment analysis, and learning from successful examples—enables you to make informed decisions that propel your business forward. Embrace these practices to cultivate a resilient, adaptive organization ready to thrive in any market environment.

Financial Forecasting: Predicting Your Path Forward

Financial forecasting is a critical skill for any entrepreneur, as it enables you to predict your path forward with greater accuracy. Making informed projections about revenues, expenses, and cash flow is essential for effective planning. Accurate forecasts not only help you allocate resources wisely but also prepare you for potential challenges. Without a clear financial roadmap, it's easy to lose sight of your goals and navigate blindly through uncertainties.

However, balancing intuition and data is equally important in this process. While numbers provide valuable insights, your instincts and experiences can also play a crucial role in decision-making. Trusting your gut can lead to innovative ideas and creative solutions, especially in situations where data may be limited or unclear. Yet, it's essential to recognize when to lean more heavily on the numbers. For instance, in high-stakes decisions like investments or budgeting, data should guide your strategy.

The key is finding harmony between intuition and data. Use your analytical skills to back your gut feelings with concrete evidence, ensuring that decisions are both instinctive and informed.

In conclusion, effective financial forecasting combined with a balanced approach to intuition and data will empower you to make strategic choices that drive your business forward. By embracing both analytical insights and personal judgment, you create a robust foundation for growth, enabling you to navigate the complexities of entrepreneurship with confidence.

Key Performance Indicators (KPIs) Every Entrepreneur Should Track

As an entrepreneur, understanding Key Performance Indicators (KPIs) is essential for evaluating the health of your business. These metrics serve as a compass, guiding your strategic decisions and helping you track progress. Some critical KPIs every entrepreneur should monitor include customer acquisition costs, revenue growth, profit margins, and customer retention rates. By keeping a close eye on these figures, you can assess how well your business is performing and identify areas for improvement.

However, one challenge many entrepreneurs face is data overload. With so much information available, it can be overwhelming to determine what truly matters. To overcome this, focus on filtering and prioritizing actionable data. Start by defining your core objectives and selecting KPIs that align with those goals. Use dashboards and visualization tools to simplify complex data sets, making it easier to spot trends and patterns that require your attention.

Benchmarking against industry standards is another effective strategy. Comparing your KPIs to those of competitors provides valuable insights into your market positioning. By understanding how your business stacks up, you can identify gaps and opportunities for growth.

In conclusion, tracking essential KPIs, overcoming data overload, and benchmarking against industry standards are vital components of a successful entrepreneurial strategy. By harnessing these practices, you empower yourself to make informed decisions that enhance your business's performance and drive sustainable growth. Embrace the power of asking for insights and guidance as you navigate the complexities of entrepreneurship.

Numbers speak louder than words; they tell a story of truth that emotions often can't capture.

CHAPTER THREE

'SELF-RELIANCE'

THE POWER OF NEVER DEPENDING ON OTHERS

The Philosophy of Self-Reliance

The philosophy of self-reliance is all about understanding the importance of being self-sufficient. In the past, I often relied on others for support and decision-making. While this seemed convenient at the time, I soon realized it left me lacking in knowledge and skills. I wasn't learning as much as I could have, and this affected my growth as an entrepreneur.

Now, I make a conscious effort to do things myself. Whether it's tackling a new project or learning a new skill, I embrace the challenge. This approach has not only increased my confidence but also equipped me with valuable knowledge. I've found that figuring things out on my own leads to deeper understanding and personal growth.

Emotional self-sufficiency is another key aspect of self-reliance. It's essential to cultivate emotional intelligence and practice self-care. This means being aware of my feelings and learning how to manage them effectively. When I take care of my emotional well-being, I can handle stress and setbacks more easily.

In summary, embracing self-reliance empowers me to take control of my journey. By learning to rely on myself and nurturing my emotional health, I've become a stronger entrepreneur. The more I depend on myself, the more capable I feel in facing challenges and achieving my goals. Remember, self-reliance isn't just about doing everything alone; it's about growing into the best version of yourself.

Cultivating Inner Strength

Cultivating inner strength is key to becoming self-reliant. It's about building resilience and confidence so that you can trust yourself. Self-reliance doesn't mean you should never ask for help; instead, it means you should not rely on others to do your work for you. Asking for help when needed is perfectly fine—it's about taking responsibility for your own journey.

I've learned that spending time alone can lead to important self-discovery. Moments of solitude allow me to reflect on my thoughts and feelings, helping me find clarity and purpose. During these quiet times, I can think about what I really want and how to achieve it. This self-reflection has been crucial for my growth as an entrepreneur.

Additionally, acquiring new skills is essential for enhancing self-reliance. I focus on identifying areas where I can improve, whether it's learning about marketing, finance, or leadership. By developing these skills, I become more independent and capable of handling challenges on my own.

In summary, self-reliance is about trusting yourself while knowing it's okay to seek help when necessary. It involves building resilience, taking time for self-reflection, and continually learning new skills. By embracing self-reliance, you empower yourself to navigate your entrepreneurial journey with confidence and strength. The more you rely on yourself, the more equipped you become to face whatever comes your way.

The Dangers of Dependency

In my journey as an entrepreneur, I've learned that dependency can be one of the biggest obstacles to personal growth. Relying on others to handle tasks often leads to unfinished work and missed opportunities. There were times when I depended too much on partners or employees to get things done, and this habit became a major setback for me.

When I relied on others, I often found that projects didn't progress as planned. Delays happened, and important decisions were left in someone else's hands. This lack of control caused frustration and disappointment. I realized that depending on others not only affected my business but also hindered my own development.

Being self-reliant means taking ownership of your work and responsibilities. It empowers you to make decisions, learn new skills, and push through challenges without waiting for someone else. By trusting myself to get things done, I've discovered my true potential and ability to complete tasks effectively.

This shift towards self-reliance has taught me the importance of managing my own responsibilities and not relying solely on others. It's okay to ask for help, but I've learned that I must also be proactive in driving my own success. Embracing self-reliance has turned my failures into lessons and opened doors to new opportunities. In the end, relying on myself has been the key to my growth and achievements as an entrepreneur.

Taking Responsibility for Your Life

I've learned that taking responsibility for my life is crucial to achieving my goals. In the past, I often relied on others to help me with tasks or to make decisions. This dependence sometimes led to unfinished projects and missed opportunities.

Now, I focus on being accountable for everything I start. When I take responsibility, I feel a sense of ownership over my work and my life. I've realized that if something goes wrong, it's up to me to fix it. This mindset shift has made a significant difference in how I approach challenges.

When I commit to completing a task, I give it my all. Whether it's a small project or a major business decision, I focus on seeing it through to the end. This dedication not only boosts my confidence but also helps me learn from my experiences. Each accomplishment, no matter how small, reinforces my belief in myself.

Taking responsibility also means being honest about my strengths and weaknesses. I assess what I can do on my own and where I might need support. However, I no longer rely on others to carry the weight for me. This shift has made me more resilient and resourceful.

Ultimately, embracing self-reliance and accountability has transformed my entrepreneurial journey, allowing me to achieve more than I ever thought possible.

Developing Problem-Solving Skills

Self-reliance is all about becoming your own problem-solver. In my experience, developing strong problem-solving skills has been crucial. It's not just about finding answers; it's about learning to think resourcefully. When faced with challenges, I've learned to break them down into smaller parts, which makes them easier to tackle. This approach has helped me feel more capable and confident.

Trusting my intuition has also played a big role in my journey. Sometimes, the best decisions come from listening to that little voice inside me. When I trust my instincts, I can navigate tricky situations more effectively. It's like having a built-in compass that guides me toward what feels right.

To strengthen these skills, I practice reflecting on past experiences. I ask myself what worked, what didn't, and what I can do differently next time. This reflection helps me grow and adapt, making me a better decision-maker.

Additionally, I keep an open mind and seek out new information. The more I learn, the more tools I have in my toolkit for solving problems. Whether it's reading books, taking courses, or talking to others, continuous learning keeps me sharp and resourceful.

By developing my problem-solving skills and trusting my intuition, I've become more self-reliant. This independence not only helps me in my business but also empowers me to face life's challenges with confidence.

Embracing Failure as a Teacher

Embracing failure has been one of the most important lessons in my journey. When things don't go as planned, I try to see those setbacks as valuable teachers. Each failure shows me what I can do differently next time. This mindset helps me become more independent because I learn to rely on my own experiences rather than waiting for others to guide me.

Financial independence is another key part of self-reliance. I focus on building my wealth by managing my resources wisely. This means creating a budget, saving for the future, and investing in opportunities that can grow my money. By being in control of my finances, I'm not dependent on anyone else for my stability. It gives me the freedom to make choices based on my own goals.

Setting personal goals is essential for my growth. I've learned to define what I want to achieve without seeking validation from others. Whether it's starting a new project or learning a new skill, I focus on my objectives. I break these goals down into smaller steps, making them easier to reach. This process not only keeps me motivated but also reinforces my belief in my own abilities.

By embracing failure, achieving financial independence, and setting my own goals, I've cultivated a strong sense of self-reliance. This journey empowers me to take charge of my life and pursue my dreams without depending on anyone else.

The Art of Self-Discipline

In my journey as an entrepreneur, I've learned that self-discipline is essential for staying focused and motivated. Setting clear goals helps me stay on track and direct my energy toward what truly matters. This commitment to self-reliance builds a strong foundation for success.

Becoming independent not only benefits me but also inspires those around me. When others see my dedication, it encourages them to pursue their own goals without waiting for help. This ripple effect can uplift an entire community.

While it's vital to be self-reliant, building a supportive environment is equally important. I surround myself with positive influences—friends and mentors who uplift me. However, I ensure this support doesn't create dependency. It's great to have guidance, but I remind myself that the ultimate responsibility lies with me.

When challenges arise, I seek advice from my network but take charge of finding solutions. This keeps me empowered and accountable for my decisions.

By mastering self-discipline and creating a positive environment, I focus on my goals while inspiring others to do the same. This balance allows me to grow as an entrepreneur while fostering independence in those around me. Embracing self-reliance truly transforms not just my journey, but the journeys of others as well.

Self-reliance is the strength to trust yourself and the courage to stand on your own, knowing that true growth comes from within.

CHAPTER FOUR

'CHOOSING THE RIGHT PARTNERS'

THE KEY TO SUSTAINABLE SUCCESS

The Importance of Strategic Partnerships

I've learned that selecting the right partners is crucial for sustainable success. Strategic partnerships can open doors and create opportunities that might otherwise remain closed. However, it's essential to step into partnerships only when necessary. Each collaboration should align with your vision and values, enhancing your business rather than complicating it.

Collaboration is not just beneficial; it's vital for long-term growth. By understanding the dynamics of partnership, you can leverage collective strengths to navigate challenges and seize opportunities. As you explore potential alliances, consider how these partnerships can be scaled for growth. Successful collaborations should allow both parties to expand into new markets and reach wider audiences.

To find the right partners, leverage your networks effectively. Attend industry events, join entrepreneurial groups, and connect with like-minded individuals. Each interaction is a chance to discover potential collaborators who share your goals and can complement your skills.

Finally, never underestimate the impact of partnership on your brand reputation. The right alliances can elevate your brand image, enhancing credibility and trust among your audience. Conversely, choosing the wrong partners can damage your reputation and undermine your efforts.

In conclusion, the art of choosing the right partners lies in careful consideration and strategic alignment. Approach partnerships with intention, and you'll pave the way for a thriving entrepreneurial journey.

Identifying Your Needs

Choosing the right partners is pivotal for achieving sustainable success. To embark on a fruitful partnership, first assess what you truly seek. Clarify your business goals and identify the specific strengths and resources you need to reach them. This self-reflection will guide you in finding partners who complement your vision.

One of the most effective strategies is to recognize your weaknesses and seek partners whose strengths can fill those gaps. For instance, if your expertise lies in product development but you struggle with marketing, aligning with a partner skilled in that area can create a powerful synergy. This mutual support not only enhances your capabilities but also fosters a balanced partnership where both parties thrive.

Once you've pinpointed your needs, evaluate whether potential partners can fulfill them. Engage in open conversations about expectations and objectives to ensure alignment. It's vital that both parties share a common vision and commitment to success.

Ultimately, a successful partnership hinges on the right fit. By carefully assessing what you seek and identifying complementary strengths, you position yourself for growth and innovation. Remember, partnerships are not just about shared goals; they are about leveraging each other's capabilities to navigate challenges and seize opportunities. When chosen wisely, the right partners can propel your business to new heights, ensuring a sustainable path forward.

Evaluating Potential Partners

I've learned that selecting the right partners is crucial for success. One significant advantage of diverse partnerships is their ability to enhance creativity and innovation. When people from different backgrounds come together, they bring unique perspectives that can spark new ideas and solutions, pushing your business to new heights.

However, it's essential to approach potential partners with caution. Trust should be earned, not given freely. Always conduct thorough research into their backgrounds and past partnership experiences. This due diligence can reveal important insights about their work ethic and reliability.

Finding the right partners is often challenging. I've experienced partnerships where one party consistently did their job while the other contributed little. Such imbalances can lead to frustration and hinder progress. It's vital to seek out partners who are equally committed to the venture. Look for individuals who not only possess complementary skills but are also willing to invest the same effort as you do.

In essence, the success of your business can hinge on the strength of your partnerships. By embracing diversity, conducting careful evaluations, and ensuring mutual commitment, you create a foundation for collaboration that fosters growth. Choose partners wisely, and you'll pave the way for a thriving entrepreneurial journey where creativity flourishes and innovation thrives.

Building Trust and Transparency

Building trust and transparency is essential in forming strong partnerships. Effective collaboration thrives on mutual respect and open communication. When partners are honest about their intentions and expectations, they create a solid foundation that supports growth and innovation.

Negotiating terms and agreements is another critical step in establishing a successful partnership. Key considerations should include defining roles, responsibilities, and financial contributions. A fair and beneficial agreement sets the tone for collaboration, ensuring that all parties feel valued and committed to the venture.

Monitoring and evaluating partnership performance is vital for maintaining a healthy relationship. Establishing metrics to assess effectiveness allows you to identify areas for improvement and celebrate successes. Regular check-ins can help address issues before they escalate and keep the partnership aligned with shared goals.

Legal considerations also play a crucial role in partnerships. Understanding the legal aspects of forming and maintaining partnerships can prevent misunderstandings and protect everyone involved. Having a clear legal framework ensures that all partners are on the same page regarding their rights and obligations.

I've experienced partnerships where a lack of transparency led to distrust and ultimately the partnership's demise. When individuals prioritize their own interests over collective success, it jeopardizes the relationship. To avoid this fate, prioritize trust, clear agreements, ongoing evaluation, and legal clarity in your partnerships. By doing so, you set the stage for a successful entrepreneurial journey built on strong, respectful collaborations

The Role of Communication

Effective communication is the cornerstone of successful partnerships. It fosters collaboration, prevents misunderstandings, and ensures that all parties are aligned on goals and expectations. In my experience, I've always prioritized open dialogue, setting aside my ego to facilitate honest conversations. This approach not only strengthens relationships but also cultivates a culture of trust, where partners feel comfortable sharing their ideas and concerns.

Continuous learning and adaptation are equally important in evolving partnerships. The business landscape is constantly changing, and successful collaborations must be agile enough to respond to new market demands. Regularly assessing and refining your partnership strategies can lead to innovative solutions and help you stay competitive. Encourage a mindset of learning among your partners, where feedback is valued, and growth is a shared objective.

By fostering effective communication and embracing continuous learning, partnerships can navigate challenges more effectively and seize opportunities that arise. I've witnessed firsthand how addressing issues early through open communication can prevent small misunderstandings from escalating into major conflicts. Moreover, adapting together as market dynamics shift can lead to enhanced creativity and resilience.

In conclusion, prioritize clear communication and a commitment to learning within your partnerships. These practices not only strengthen the foundation of your collaboration but also empower you to thrive in an ever-changing business environment. By nurturing a culture of openness and adaptability, you'll create partnerships that are not only sustainable but also fruitful.

Handling Conflicts and Challenges

Handling conflicts and challenges is an inevitable part of any partnership. In my experience, I've always aimed to avoid conflicts, believing that open communication could prevent misunderstandings. However, I've learned that conflict resolution isn't always straightforward, especially when a partner is reluctant to acknowledge their mistakes. In such situations, it's crucial to remain calm and focus on the facts rather than emotions. Address the issue directly, emphasizing the importance of transparency and accountability for maintaining a healthy relationship.

When disagreements arise, using effective conflict resolution strategies can make a significant difference. Actively listen to your partner's perspective, and express your own concerns clearly and respectfully. Finding common ground can help you navigate the disagreement and reinforce the partnership.

Additionally, it's wise to evaluate exit strategies before conflicts escalate. Preparing for the possibility of ending a partnership can ensure a smooth transition if the relationship no longer serves both parties. Discussing exit terms upfront fosters transparency and trust, allowing both partners to understand their rights and obligations should the need arise.

Ultimately, the goal is to maintain strong relationships, even in the face of challenges. By approaching conflicts with a collaborative mindset and planning for potential exits, you can safeguard your entrepreneurial journey. Remember, how you handle difficulties can define the strength and longevity of your partnerships, paving the way for future successes.

Sustainability in Partnerships

Choosing the right partners is crucial for transforming a small business into a successful enterprise. In my experience, it's essential to select partners who not only contribute positively to your vision but also alleviate burdens rather than adding to them. The ideal partner should bring complementary skills, resources, and insights that help elevate your business without overwhelming you with additional responsibilities.

Aligning business practices with sustainability goals is another key factor for long-term success. As the market increasingly values environmentally responsible practices, having partners who share this commitment can enhance your brand's reputation and open new opportunities. Sustainable practices not only attract customers but also foster innovation and resilience in your business model.

Cultural fit is equally important in partnership dynamics. Ensuring that your partners share similar values and objectives creates a unified vision, making collaboration more seamless. When partners are aligned in their mission and ethics, it strengthens the foundation of the relationship and boosts overall productivity. Discrepancies in values can lead to misunderstandings and conflicts that undermine progress.

In conclusion, when choosing partners, focus on those who can help you scale your business while sharing your sustainability goals and cultural values. By building a network of like-minded collaborators, you set the stage for a thriving entrepreneurial journey that benefits not just your business but the community and environment as well. This alignment is essential for lasting success.

Choosing the wrong partners can turn a dream into a nightmare; the right alliances should lift you up, not weigh you down.

CHAPTER FIVE

'SEPARATE THE NOISE'

BUSINESS FEEDBACK MATTERS, NOT OPINIONS ABOUT OTHERS

The Weight of Opinions: Friends vs. Feedback

In our lives, we often struggle to separate personal opinions from constructive feedback, leading to confusion and frustration. This blending can weigh us down, especially when we seek validation from friends rather than genuine advice. To thrive, it's crucial to understand the difference between the two.

Friends often share their thoughts based on feelings, which can sometimes cloud the truth. While their support is valuable, it may not always be grounded in reality. On the other hand, useful feedback is aimed at helping us improve, focusing on specific actions and outcomes rather than personal judgments.

I've experienced this firsthand. I frequently felt overwhelmed by what others thought about me and my business. Instead of taking their words as potential lessons, I reacted defensively, believing they were criticizing me personally. This response only added to my frustration.

Over time, I learned to distinguish between the opinions of friends and constructive feedback. By actively listening to what people had to say without taking it personally, I began to see the value in their insights. I realized that feedback could guide my growth and decision-making rather than define me.

This shift in perspective transformed my approach. I learned to embrace feedback as a tool for improvement, freeing myself from the weight of unhelpful opinions. By understanding this difference, I found clarity and confidence in my professional journey, enabling me to focus on what truly matters.

Noise from Loved Ones: Recognizing Bias

Navigating feedback from loved ones can be challenging, especially when emotional connections introduce bias. In my experience, I often turned to those I trusted, believing their insights would be valuable. However, I eventually realized that many of the people I admired used my situation as a source of entertainment, offering feedback based on their perspectives rather than genuine experience.

This realization was eye-opening. I found that even the closest friends and family members could be influenced by their feelings and biases. Their opinions were shaped by how others viewed me, leading to feedback that wasn't always constructive. I learned that every loved one has their own biases, which can skew their advice.

To find more reliable feedback, I began seeking insights from a broader circle, focusing on those who I believed would provide honest and thoughtful opinions. It became clear that not everyone was equipped to give unbiased advice, regardless of their good intentions.

It's important to be selective about whom you turn to for feedback. Choosing the right people—whether family or friends—can significantly impact your business and personal relationships. If you receive biased advice and act on it, it can harm both your work and your connections.

Ultimately, it's crucial to filter the noise and seek out those who will provide genuine feedback. This helps you make informed decisions without being swayed by emotional influences. By being mindful of the sources of feedback, you can protect your relationships and stay focused on what truly matters.

Distancing personal relationships from business decisions.

In my journey as an entrepreneur, one critical lesson I've learned is the importance of cultivating an objective mindset by separating personal relationships from business decisions. Mixing the two can lead to confusion and distraction, ultimately derailing your focus and vision. When emotions get involved, it's easy to lose sight of your goals.

Feedback from friends and family can be well-intentioned but often comes with inherent biases. Their opinions may be influenced by personal feelings rather than objective insights that can genuinely help your business. While it's important to listen to those you care about, relying solely on their viewpoints can distort your decision-making process.

To maintain clarity, I've implemented several techniques. First, I set clear boundaries between my personal and professional lives. This means being intentional about when and how I seek feedback from loved ones, ensuring I don't get sidetracked by their emotional responses.

Additionally, I actively seek out feedback from diverse sources, including mentors and industry peers who can provide unbiased, constructive insights. This approach allows me to gather well-rounded perspectives without the emotional noise that often clouds judgment.

Ultimately, focusing on business feedback rather than personal opinions helps me make informed decisions that benefit my entrepreneurial journey. By separating the noise, I can navigate challenges with confidence and keep my vision clear, safeguarding both my business and my relationships.

Filtering Feedback: What Truly Matters

Understanding the difference between feedback and opinion is crucial for success. Feedback refers to constructive insights aimed at improving your work, while opinions are often subjective viewpoints that may not serve your goals. The challenge lies in filtering these inputs effectively to identify what truly matters.

To navigate this, I've learned to assess feedback based on its relevance to my business needs. I prioritize constructive criticism that can help me grow while setting aside opinions that don't contribute to my vision. I often joke that I use one ear to listen and the other to let go of unnecessary noise.

Negative feedback can be particularly harmful. If you dwell on it, it can feel like poison, draining your motivation and interest. I've found myself trapped in this cycle before, feeling hopeless and stuck. Instead, I've learned to use feedback as a source of motivation, transforming challenges into opportunities for growth.

Remember, people offer feedback when they notice something worth discussing. It's essential to focus on insights that can propel you forward rather than getting bogged down by irrelevant opinions. By filtering out the noise and concentrating on valuable feedback, you can maintain clarity and drive in your entrepreneurial journey, ultimately leading to success without unnecessary distractions.

The Art of Asking the Right Questions

In my experience, one crucial aspect of receiving valuable feedback is mastering the art of asking the right questions. We often have numerous questions swirling in our minds, hoping for insightful answers. Yet, too frequently, we end up receiving responses that do little to help us.

When I started my resort in Shimla, I faced a barrage of negative feedback that left me disheartened. Similarly, when I launched a laundry business, the mixed opinions I received led me to lose interest entirely. I realized I was seeking validation for my ideas, even when I knew deep down that the path might be challenging.

To foster a positive mindset, it's essential to ask the right questions. This means approaching the right people—those with relevant experience and insights—rather than seeking opinions from those who lack expertise or interest in your field.

What's the point of asking business-related questions to someone who doesn't understand the industry? Instead, I learned to target my inquiries, focusing on individuals who could provide constructive feedback. This shift allowed me to gather insights that truly mattered, empowering me to make informed decisions.

Ultimately, the quality of the questions you ask directly impacts the quality of the feedback you receive. By honing this skill, you can navigate your entrepreneurial journey with greater clarity and confidence, filtering out the noise and focusing on what truly drives success.

Learning to Say No to Opinions

One of the most important lessons I've learned is the art of saying no to unsolicited opinions. I've found that many well-meaning suggestions from loved ones can lead to confusion and misdirection. Unfortunately, I've ruined potential deals by allowing these opinions to sway my decisions, and at times, I've regretted not pursuing opportunities that could have led to success.

I think setting boundaries around unsolicited advice is crucial. It's essential to filter out opinions that don't align with your business vision. I've learned to say no to advice that reflects personal biases rather than constructive feedback. This distinction has been vital in preserving my focus and clarity.

Controlling my thoughts has also been key. I realized that accepting unwanted opinions can clutter my mind and hinder my decision-making. By consciously choosing which voices to listen to, I've been able to concentrate on the feedback that truly matters—insights that align with my goals and aspirations.

In this process, I've gained a greater understanding of the importance of surrounding myself with individuals who offer valuable perspectives rather than opinions. By filtering out the noise and honing in on meaningful feedback, I can navigate my business journey with confidence and purpose. Saying no to unsolicited opinions has empowered me to make decisions that are authentic to my vision, ultimately driving my success forward.

Building a Feedback Network

One of the most valuable lessons I've learned is the importance of building a strong feedback network. Early on, I often relied on the opinions of friends and family, which led me astray. I quickly realized that their insights, while well-meaning, lacked the industry expertise I needed.

Before launching any business, I now prioritize seeking advice from experienced mentors. I learned this the hard way after facing losses in several ventures due to my reluctance to reach out for guidance. I entered markets without the crucial insights that only experts could provide, and those missteps were costly.

Recognizing the need for knowledgeable advisors, I began actively connecting with professionals within my industry. I sought out mentors who had faced similar challenges and could offer unbiased feedback based on real experience. This shift has kept me focused and minimized the risk of failure.

As I continue to build my network, I am constantly on the lookout for people who can share their expertise and insights. This proactive approach not only enhances my decision-making but also reinforces the importance of seeking guidance from those who truly understand the landscape.

By surrounding myself with knowledgeable mentors, I have gained the confidence to navigate my entrepreneurial path. Their insights have become the foundation of my success, guiding me toward informed decisions that align with my goals. Ultimately, I urge fellow entrepreneurs to prioritize building their feedback networks; it can make all the difference in achieving lasting success.

Let go of unwanted opinions; they cloud your vision. Embrace constructive feedback—it's the spark that fuels your growth.

CHAPTER SIX

'BUILT TO LAST'

AVOIDING THE TRAP OF SHORT-TERM GAINS AND QUICK SCAMS

Understanding the Long Game

In my journey through entrepreneurship, I quickly learned the critical difference between short-term gains and long-term success. Early on, I fell into the trap of chasing the latest trends, mistaking them for legitimate opportunities. One particular venture taught me a hard but valuable lesson. I was drawn to a market buzz that seemed promising, expecting it to yield quick profits. However, when the excitement fizzled, so did my business, revealing that I had been lured into what was essentially a short-term scam.

This experience became a turning point. I realized the importance of discerning hype from genuine opportunity. Scams and fleeting trends often appear appealing because they promise immediate rewards, but they rarely contribute to sustainable success. From that point onward, I developed a more cautious approach, creating a set of criteria to evaluate new ventures. I asked myself if each opportunity aligned with my long-term vision and if it had the potential to create lasting value.

This shift in perspective was crucial. The long game, I discovered, requires patience, careful planning, and a commitment to building something that endures. Short-term scams, on the other hand, are designed to exploit immediate excitement while distracting from the fundamental changes driving real market success.

To avoid being misled, I started paying more attention to genuine customer feedback and real market trends rather than being swayed by hype. I learned that success isn't about quick wins or appealing to the crowd—it's about staying true to your values and focusing on what truly creates long-term value. This clarity empowered me to make smarter decisions and pursue sustainable growth with confidence, avoiding the pitfalls of short-term distractions.

The Allure of Quick Wins

In the world of entrepreneurship, the allure of quick wins can be intoxicating. Short-term gains promise immediate rewards, but they often come with hidden dangers. As I navigated my entrepreneurial journey, I found that the temptation to chase these fleeting rewards can lead to a cycle of instability and regret.

Recognizing scams and get-rich-quick schemes is crucial. Common indicators include exaggerated promises, lack of transparency, and pressure to act quickly. These red flags serve as warnings, reminding us that genuine success is rarely a sprint but rather a marathon requiring patience and perseverance.

The cost of instant gratification is high. I experienced this firsthand when my focus on immediate rewards led me to neglect foundational growth. Seeking quick rewards can undermine long-term potential, stunting the very progress we aim to achieve.

Furthermore, it's vital to differentiate between trends and lasting changes in the market. While trends may provide temporary excitement, they often lack the sustainability necessary for enduring success.

Financial discipline is key for long-term gains. Implementing best practices for budgeting and investment not only secures immediate needs but also lays a solid foundation for future growth.

In conclusion, building a lasting enterprise requires a commitment to patience, discernment, and strategic planning. Avoiding the traps of quick gains can pave the way for sustained success, ensuring that our entrepreneurial ventures are built to last.

The Power of Patience

Patience is a virtue that can make or break an entrepreneur. Early in my career, I learned this the hard way. Like many,

I was lured by promises of quick returns. A friend once approached me with an investment opportunity that seemed too good to be true. The potential profits were staggering, but something felt off. In my eagerness, I ignored my instincts.

Scammers thrive on urgency; they don't give you time to think. They want you to jump in without questioning. "Why isn't this person doing it themselves if it's so profitable?" I should have asked. Instead, I rushed in, driven by the allure of easy money. Unfortunately, I ended up losing my investment, a costly lesson in the importance of patience.

As I reflected on my experience, I realized how many others, including friends, had fallen into similar traps due to a lack of foresight. The businesses that truly thrive are those built on perseverance and careful consideration. Case studies of successful entrepreneurs who waited and planned strategically inspired me. They understood that sustainable growth takes time.

Now, I approach every opportunity with caution. I analyze whether it's a short-term gamble or a long-term investment. By prioritizing patience, I've learned to differentiate between genuine opportunities and fleeting scams. Success isn't about rushing; it's about understanding the landscape and allowing your vision to unfold over time.

Long-Term Strategy vs. Short-Term Tactics

In entrepreneurship, it's crucial to understand the difference between long-term strategy and short-term tactics. While quick decisions may seem tempting for immediate results, they can lead to mistakes, including falling for scams. I've learned that keeping a focus on long-term goals is essential for sustainable growth.

It's also important to recognize people or opportunities that might be scams. Often, the promise of quick money hides dangerous intentions. Trust your instincts and be cautious, especially with those who prioritize fast profits over solid foundations. A good long-term strategy helps you make smart choices and avoid risky situations.

True success in business isn't just about making money. It involves measuring your impact, sticking to your values, and ensuring your business is sustainable. When you think about success this way, you build a brand that connects with customers and creates a lasting impression.

By focusing on long-term goals, you build trust and loyalty among your audience. A commitment to planning helps you navigate challenges with confidence and avoid quick traps.

In short, balancing long-term vision with short-term actions keeps your business focused on what really matters—making a positive impact and being sustainable. This approach ensures that your entrepreneurial journey stands the test of time.

Financial Discipline for Long-Term Gains

Financial discipline is the cornerstone of long-term success in entrepreneurship. I learned this lesson the hard way when I fell victim to a Ponzi scheme, losing around 64 lakhs—one of my biggest regrets. A Ponzi scam lures investors with promises of high returns, using funds from new investors to pay earlier ones, creating an illusion of profitability. Unfortunately, when the scheme collapses, many, including myself, are left devastated.

What struck me most was the silence of those I cared about, people I thought would support me in my journey. Their absence during my crisis underscored the importance of financial prudence and choosing trustworthy opportunities.

To avoid similar pitfalls, implementing best practices for budgeting and investment is essential. Establishing a strong foundation involves understanding essential principles of a resilient business model, such as consistent cash flow and clear value propositions.

Moreover, striking the right balance between diversification and speculation is crucial. Diversifying your investments helps mitigate risks while avoiding the temptations of quick scams. Instead of chasing immediate gains, focus on strategies that promote steady growth over time.

In conclusion, building a sustainable business requires vigilance, patience, and a commitment to sound financial practices. By avoiding the allure of quick wins, we can cultivate ventures that truly stand the test of time, ensuring that our efforts are built to last.

Learning from Failure

Learning from failure became my guiding principle after I faced a significant financial loss. Initially, the weight of disappointment felt overwhelming, and I struggled not to let it drag me down. But rather than wallowing in despair, I sought inspiration from motivational speakers who encouraged resilience and the importance of setbacks.

To clear my mind, I started to sit in my laundry business. It was a welcome distraction, but more importantly, it provided me with the chance to observe how a steady operation thrived. As I worked, I found myself analyzing my past mistakes, questioning how I had allowed myself to get trapped in ventures that promised quick returns but delivered nothing but disappointment.

Through this reflection, I discovered a crucial lesson: each failure was a stepping stone, packed with insights that could inform my future strategies. I learned to be wary of anything that resembled a scam or relied solely on short-term gains. My experiences taught me to prioritize long-term sustainability over fleeting success.

Now, when faced with new opportunities, I approach them with caution and discernment. I've built a mental checklist, always asking if an opportunity aligns with my long-term vision. Embracing my failures has transformed my mindset. Instead of fearing setbacks, I now view them as essential parts of my growth, driving me toward resilience and informed decision-making in my entrepreneurial journey.

Ethical Business Practices

Business practices are the bedrock of sustainable entrepreneurship. In a landscape where many prioritize money over ethics, maintaining integrity is not just a choice—it's a necessity. I've witnessed how the pursuit of profit can tempt individuals to compromise their values, ultimately jeopardizing their long-term success. Choosing ethics fosters trust, both within your team and with your customers, laying the groundwork for a lasting legacy.

Integrity plays a pivotal role in building a business that endures. When your stakeholders see that you prioritize ethical behaviour, they are more likely to engage with and support your mission. This trust can become a powerful differentiator in a crowded marketplace.

Moreover, embracing innovation is crucial for staying relevant while adhering to your core mission. Change is inevitable, but it should enhance—not dilute—your ethical standards. By welcoming new ideas and approaches, you can adapt to evolving market conditions while remaining true to your values.

Creating a legacy involves deliberate strategies that ensure your business leaves a lasting impact. This means aligning your operations with ethical practices, investing in community initiatives, and prioritizing sustainability. When your business prioritizes ethics, you not only contribute positively to society but also create a brand that resonates with future generations.

In essence, by embedding ethics into your entrepreneurial journey, you pave the way for a resilient business that stands the test of time, ensuring your efforts are built to last.

~

*Scams don't chase you, They come
for your greed or need*

~

CHAPTER SEVEN

'MASTERING THE MULTITASK'

WHY AUTOMATION IS KEY TO MANAGING MULTIPLE BUSINESSES

The Multitasking Challenge

Managing multiple ventures simultaneously presents a unique set of challenges for entrepreneurs. The multitasking challenge is not just about juggling various responsibilities; it's about understanding the complexities that come with each business's distinct needs. Each venture requires attention, strategy, and resources, and without a structured approach, it's easy to feel overwhelmed.

One of the most significant complexities lies in resource allocation. When you're stretched thin across multiple businesses, prioritizing tasks becomes essential. Each venture demands different levels of attention, and determining where to focus your efforts can be daunting. This is where automation plays a pivotal role. By automating routine tasks such as customer follow-ups, inventory management, and financial reporting, you can streamline operations and free up time for strategic decision-making.

Furthermore, effective communication is vital. With teams spread across different projects, maintaining clarity and alignment is challenging. Automating communication channels—like setting up automated updates or reminders—ensures that everyone is informed and engaged without overwhelming yourself with constant oversight.

Lastly, embracing a mindset of adaptability is crucial. The landscape of entrepreneurship is ever-changing, and being able to pivot quickly while managing multiple ventures is a skill that comes with experience.

In conclusion, mastering the multitasking challenge involves recognizing the complexities of managing various businesses. By leveraging automation and prioritizing effectively, you can navigate these challenges, ensuring each venture thrives while maintaining your own well-being. Embrace these strategies to turn multitasking into a strength rather than a source of stress.

Defining Automation

In the world of entrepreneurship, especially when managing multiple businesses, defining automation becomes crucial. Automation refers to the use of technology to perform repetitive tasks without human intervention, allowing entrepreneurs to streamline operations across various ventures. This can include automating processes like customer inquiries, inventory tracking, and financial reporting. Understanding automation in this context is key to achieving efficiency and scalability.

The benefits of automation in a multi-business environment are significant. First and foremost, it enhances efficiency. By automating routine tasks, you free up valuable time and resources, enabling you to focus on strategic initiatives rather than getting bogged down by day-to-day operations. This is particularly vital when juggling several ventures, as it allows for better oversight and management without the risk of burnout.

Moreover, automation significantly reduces errors. Human error is an inherent risk in manual processes, particularly in data entry and calculations. Automated systems minimize these risks, ensuring greater accuracy and consistency across your businesses. This not only improves operational reliability but also enhances customer satisfaction and trust.

In conclusion, mastering the multitask involves a solid understanding of automation and its benefits. By leveraging automation to enhance efficiency and reduce errors, you create a more streamlined and effective operational framework for your multiple businesses. Embrace automation as a powerful ally in your entrepreneurial journey, and seek the necessary tools and resources to implement it successfully across your ventures.

Balancing Human Touch and Automation

In the fast-paced world of entrepreneurship, especially when managing multiple businesses, striking the right balance between human touch and automation is crucial. While automation streamlines operations and enhances efficiency, it's essential to recognize when personal interaction is necessary. Certain situations demand empathy, understanding, and human connection—elements that automation cannot replicate. For instance, handling customer complaints or negotiating partnerships often require a personal touch to build trust and rapport.

Knowing when to automate and when to engage personally can significantly impact your ventures. Automating routine tasks—such as appointment scheduling, email responses, and order confirmations—frees up valuable time, allowing you to focus on high-level strategic decisions and relationship-building. However, ensuring that key interactions, especially those involving sensitive issues, remain personal can strengthen customer loyalty and foster a positive company culture.

Streamlining communication processes is another vital aspect of automation in multi-business management. Implementing automated communication tools can improve collaboration and response times across your teams. For instance, using chatbots for initial inquiries can provide quick responses to common questions while allowing team members to handle more complex issues.

In summary, mastering the multitask requires a thoughtful approach to balancing automation with human interaction. By strategically automating routine processes while prioritizing personal engagement where it matters most, you can enhance operational efficiency and strengthen relationships across your multiple ventures. This balance ultimately leads to a more successful and sustainable business landscape.

Scaling Operations with Automation

As an entrepreneur juggling multiple businesses, scaling operations is key to growth, and automation can be a powerful ally in this process. Simply put, automation uses technology to handle repetitive tasks, making it easier to manage increasing workloads without needing more resources. This means you can grow your businesses while keeping quality high and staying efficient.

However, many entrepreneurs hesitate to embrace automation due to fears and misconceptions. Some worry that it will replace jobs or make customer interactions feel impersonal. It's important to understand that automation isn't about taking away jobs; rather, it's about freeing up time for your team to focus on more valuable tasks. When routine work is automated, employees can concentrate on strategy and creativity, which can boost morale and productivity.

To successfully adopt automation, start by identifying the repetitive tasks that consume too much time. Look for simple processes you can automate, and gradually introduce these tools. Providing training can help ease concerns and show your team the benefits of automation. Encourage open discussions about any worries they may have.

In summary, mastering multitasking means recognizing how automation can help your business grow while addressing fears about it. By using automation wisely, you can improve efficiency and create a strong foundation for success across all your ventures.

Customer Relationship Management (CRM) Automation

As an entrepreneur managing multiple businesses, automating customer interactions is a smart way to improve service and keep customers coming back. Automation tools can help you handle inquiries, send follow-up emails, and provide support without needing constant human input. This means your customers get quick responses, which enhances their experience.

Choosing the right tools is crucial for effective automation. There are various software options for different business functions, from customer relationship management (CRM) systems to chatbots for instant messaging. Research and pick tools that fit your specific needs, ensuring they integrate smoothly with your existing processes.

Marketing automation is another powerful strategy. You can automate email campaigns to reach customers at the right time, post on social media without manual effort, and generate leads automatically. This helps you maintain consistent communication with your audience while saving time.

Data analysis is also important. Automating the collection and analysis of data allows you to make informed decisions quickly. You can track sales, customer behaviour, and marketing performance without spending hours sifting through spreadsheets.

Finally, project management tools can help keep your team on track. Automation in project tracking means everyone knows their tasks and deadlines, improving collaboration and efficiency.

In summary, mastering multitasking involves using automation to enhance customer interactions, streamline marketing, analyze data, and manage projects. By embracing these tools, you can improve service and drive growth across your businesses.

Financial and Time Management Through Automation

As an entrepreneur managing multiple businesses, mastering financial and time management through automation is essential for success. I used to struggle with keeping everything organized, but I learned that automation can help streamline these processes significantly.

One key technique is using automation to optimize your schedule and priorities. For example, calendar tools can automatically set reminders for important deadlines, helping you stay on top of your tasks without constant manual input. This way, you can focus on what truly matters for your businesses.

Another vital area is automating financial tasks. Tools for invoicing, payroll, and expense tracking can save you a lot of time. Instead of spending hours on these tasks each month, automation can handle them efficiently. For instance, you can set up automatic invoicing to send out bills at regular intervals, ensuring you get paid on time.

Identifying repetitive tasks is also crucial. Look at your daily activities and find those that take up too much time, like data entry or expense tracking. These are prime candidates for automation. By automating these tasks, you can free up hours each week to focus on strategic decisions and growth.

In summary, by embracing automation for financial and time management, you can enhance your productivity and reduce stress. With the right tools and techniques, you can streamline your operations, making it easier to master multitasking and drive success in your entrepreneurial journey.

Maintaining Quality Control

Maintaining quality control is essential when you implement automation in your businesses. While automation can make processes more efficient, ensuring that quality remains consistent is critical. Customers want high standards, and any drop in quality can hurt your reputation.

One effective way to uphold quality in automated processes is by setting clear guidelines. For example, if you use chatbots for customer service, make sure they have accurate information to provide. Regularly review and update their responses to reflect current policies and product details. This helps avoid miscommunication and keeps customers satisfied.

In manufacturing, automated production lines can benefit from quality monitoring systems. For instance, using sensors can help detect defects during production. If a problem arises, you can address it immediately, ensuring only top-quality products reach your customers. This proactive approach is crucial for maintaining standards.

Regular audits of your automated processes are also necessary. Schedule these reviews to check whether your tools are performing correctly and meeting quality benchmarks. This allows you to identify and fix issues before they impact your customers.

In conclusion, ensuring quality control in automated processes is vital for customer satisfaction and long-term success. By establishing clear guidelines, employing monitoring tools, and conducting regular assessments, you can maintain the high standards your customers expect, fostering loyalty and supporting growth in your ventures.

Automation is key to managing multiple businesses, but step into it carefully; the right systems can simplify your path to success.

CHAPTER EIGHT

'CLICKS OVER FOOTSTEPS'

ELEVATING BUSINESS THROUGH DIGITAL PRESENCE

The Digital Shift: Why Online Presence Matters More Than Ever

In my journey as an entrepreneur, I've learned that having a strong online presence is crucial. The digital shift means that more people are shopping and seeking services online than ever before. In my early days, I underestimated this shift and focused too much on physical stores. As a result, I lost potential customers who were looking for my products online. Now, I realize that a robust online presence is essential for reaching today's consumers.

Understanding the customer journey is also vital. Mapping out how your audience interacts with your business online helps you create a better experience for them. When I started paying attention to this, I noticed that small changes, like improving my website's layout or simplifying the checkout process, made a big difference in customer satisfaction. It's about making their journey as smooth as possible.

Sustainability is another key factor in the digital world. Customers today care about eco-friendly practices, and I've seen this firsthand. When I shifted my focus to sustainable business practices, not only did I attract more customers, but I also felt good about the positive impact on the environment.

In summary, embracing the digital shift, understanding your audience, and committing to sustainability is essential for success today. My past failures taught me these lessons, and they now guide my approach in this ever-evolving landscape.

Building Your Brand Online: Essentials for a Strong Digital Identity

Building a strong brand online is essential for success in today's digital world. Early in my entrepreneurial journey, I struggled with my brand identity. I realized that a clear and professional online presence helps customers recognize and trust your business. It's not just about having a website; it's about showcasing what makes your brand unique.

E-commerce is another vital area. Turning clicks into sales isn't always easy, but I learned that having a user-friendly website is crucial. My first attempts at selling online were messy, and I lost many potential customers due to complicated checkout processes. Now, I focus on making it simple for people to buy, which has significantly improved my sales.

Email marketing has also been a game-changer for me. In the beginning, I didn't realize how effective it could be in building relationships with customers. Sending regular updates and offers helps keep your brand in their minds. It's all about creating connections that lead to sales.

Finally, online reviews matter. I've seen how positive reviews can boost trust and credibility. When I started encouraging satisfied customers to leave feedback, I noticed a big difference in new customers' willingness to try my products.

In summary, building your brand online, mastering e-commerce, using email marketing, and leveraging reviews are all keys to turning your digital presence into success. My past failures taught me these lessons, and now I embrace them every day.

Social Media Strategies: Choosing the Right Platforms for Your Business

Creating engaging content is crucial in today's crowded online space. In my early days, I often overlooked this, focusing more on just getting my message out there. I quickly learned that capturing attention requires creativity and relevance. Posts that resonate with your audience lead to better engagement and, ultimately, sales.

Influencer marketing became another key strategy for me. Collaborating with influencers can expand your reach significantly. At first, I hesitated to partner with others, thinking I could do it all myself. However, I realized that influencers have loyal followers who trust their recommendations. When I finally reached out for collaborations, I saw a noticeable boost in my audience.

Understanding SEO basics has also been a game-changer. Early on, my website wasn't showing up in searches, and I didn't understand why. After learning about keywords and search rankings, I made some changes that improved my online visibility. Now, I focus on optimizing my content so that potential customers can easily find me.

Finally, I discovered the power of video. Initially, I thought video content was too complicated, but I learned it's one of the best ways to engage your audience. Sharing my story through videos allowed people to connect with my brand on a personal level.

In summary, creating engaging content, leveraging influencer marketing, mastering SEO, and using video storytelling have all transformed my business. My past failures taught me these lessons, and now I embrace them to connect with my audience.

Embracing AI: Tools to Enhance Customer Experience and Efficiency

Embracing AI has been a game-changer for my business. In the past, I struggled with managing customer inquiries efficiently. That's when I realized that using AI tools could greatly enhance customer experience and improve my overall efficiency. AI helps automate routine tasks, allowing me to focus on more important aspects of my business.

One of the best tools I discovered was chatbots. Initially, I was sceptical about using them, thinking they might feel impersonal. However, I quickly learned that chatbots can provide immediate responses to customer questions, improving service and satisfaction. Customers appreciate getting quick answers, even outside business hours, and chatbots can handle many inquiries at once, saving me time and effort.

Implementing chatbots also freed up my team to focus on complex customer issues that require a human touch. This balance between automation and personal interaction has led to happier customers and a more efficient workflow. I found that the right chatbot can answer common questions, guide users through the purchasing process, and even gather feedback, all while making customers feel heard.

By embracing AI and chatbots, I've seen significant improvements in customer engagement and satisfaction. My past experiences taught me the value of these tools, and now I rely on them to keep my business running smoothly. Overall, integrating AI has not only streamlined my operations but also strengthened my connection with customers.

Remote Work and Digital Collaboration: Tools for a New Era

Remote work has transformed the way we do business, and I've learned a lot from this shift. In my past experiences, managing a team was often challenging, especially when everyone was in different locations.

However, I discovered that using the right digital collaboration tools can make a huge difference. Platforms like Zoom, Slack, and Trello have helped me communicate better with my team, track projects, and stay organized, no matter where we are.

These tools not only improve productivity but also create a sense of connection among team members. We can share ideas, celebrate small wins, and stay aligned on our goals, all from the comfort of our own spaces.

Additionally, building an online community around my brand has been essential. Engaging with customers through social media and forums allows me to foster loyalty and create lasting relationships. I've learned that people want to feel connected, so I actively encourage feedback and interaction. This helps me understand their needs and improve my offerings.

By creating a space where customers can share their experiences and ideas, I've built a supportive community that feels valued. This sense of belonging not only boosts customer loyalty but also turns them into brand advocates. Overall, embracing remote work and digital collaboration has not only improved my team's efficiency but also strengthened my connection with customers, paving the way for future success.

Bridging Traditional and Digital: Integrating Old-School Methods with New Technologies

Integrating traditional methods with new technologies has been a game-changer in my entrepreneurial journey.

In the past, I relied heavily on old-school approaches, like face-to-face meetings and paper-based marketing. While these methods have their value, I learned that embracing digital tools can enhance my business without losing the personal touch.

For example, I used to spend hours networking at events, but now I combine that with online platforms. I still attend local meetups but also connect with people on LinkedIn and other social media. This mix allows me to expand my network beyond my immediate area and reach potential customers or partners globally.

In marketing, I once relied on print ads and flyers. Now, I compliment those with digital campaigns. Email marketing and social media advertising let me target specific audiences and measure the results quickly. This way, I can see what works and adjust my strategies accordingly.

The key is to find a balance. I still value personal interactions and the trust they build, but I also leverage technology to streamline processes. For example, using customer relationship management (CRM) software helps me keep track of interactions and follow-ups more efficiently.

By bridging the gap between traditional and digital methods, I've created a more robust and effective business strategy. This blend allows me to stay relevant in a fast-changing world while maintaining the core values that got me here in the first place. Ultimately, it's about using the best of both worlds to drive success.

Future Trends: What's Next for Digital Business Growth?

As I reflect on my journey, it's clear that the future of digital business growth is both exciting and full of possibilities. One major trend is the increasing use of artificial intelligence (AI). Businesses are using AI to improve customer service and streamline operations. For example, chatbots can answer customer questions 24/7, making it easier for customers to get help anytime they need it.

Another trend is the rise of personalized marketing. Consumers expect brands to understand their preferences and offer tailored experiences. Companies can use data analytics to track customer behaviour and provide targeted ads, making marketing more effective.

Social media will continue to play a crucial role in business growth. Platforms like Instagram, Shorts, and Facebook are not just for socializing; they are powerful tools for reaching potential customers. Engaging content, such as videos and stories, helps brands connect with their audience in a meaningful way.

E-commerce is also evolving. More businesses are adopting online shopping, and features like augmented reality (AR) allow customers to try products virtually before buying. This makes online shopping more interactive and enjoyable.

Finally, sustainability is becoming a key focus. Customers want to support businesses that are eco-friendly. Companies that prioritize sustainable practices will likely stand out and gain customer loyalty.

In summary, the future of digital business growth is all about leveraging technology, personalizing experiences, and focusing on sustainability. By staying ahead of these trends, entrepreneurs can build stronger, more successful businesses.

Clicks over footsteps remind us that in today's world, a strong digital presence can create more connections and opportunities than traditional paths ever could.

CHAPTER NINE

'INVESTING VS. BUILDING'

UNDERSTANDING THE DISTINCT WORLDS OF BUSINESS AND INVESTMENT

Defining Investment and Business Building

Understanding the difference between investing and building a business has been crucial in my entrepreneurial journey. Investing often involves putting money into existing businesses or assets, hoping they will grow in value. In contrast, building a business means creating something from scratch, managing every detail, and nurturing it to success. I've learned this distinction through my own experiences, including failures that taught me hard lessons about each approach.

When evaluating opportunities, the criteria I use for business ideas and investments are quite different. For a business, I consider factors like my passion, market demand, and what unique value I can offer. For investments, I focus more on the potential return and the stability of the business I'm investing in. I once jumped into an investment without thoroughly assessing the business model, and it cost me. This taught me to look deeper before committing my money.

Networking has played a vital role in both areas. In business building, relationships help me find mentors, collaborators, and customers. These connections are often built through shared experiences and mutual goals. In investing, the focus is more on networking with other investors and financial experts who can provide insights and opportunities. I realized that while both fields rely on connections, the nature of those relationships differs significantly.

By understanding these distinctions, I can make better decisions and avoid repeating past mistakes. Each experience has shaped my approach to both investing and building, helping me navigate the business world more effectively.

Mindsets of Investors vs. Entrepreneurs

In my journey, I've noticed that the mindsets of investors and entrepreneurs are quite different, shaped by their unique goals and experiences. Investors often think in terms of numbers, focusing on potential returns and risks.

They analyze data and market trends to decide where to put their money. On the other hand, entrepreneurs are driven by passion and creativity. They envision building something meaningful, often willing to take risks to turn their ideas into reality. I've learned this distinction through my own failures, where I sometimes focused too much on the investment side without embracing the entrepreneurial spirit.

Innovation plays a crucial role in both areas, but in different ways. Entrepreneurs constantly seek new ideas and solutions to improve their businesses. They are the ones who innovate, taking risks to create products or services that meet customer needs. I experienced this firsthand when I launched a product that didn't resonate with the market. It taught me the importance of understanding my customers and adapting quickly.

Investors, meanwhile, look for innovative companies to support. They want to invest in businesses that show promise and can disrupt the market. I once invested in a company without fully understanding its innovation strategy, which led to losses. This taught me the importance of aligning with entrepreneurs who have a clear vision and innovative approach.

By understanding these mindsets, I've become better at navigating the worlds of both investing and building, using my past experiences to guide my decisions.

Risk Tolerance: A Key Difference

One of the biggest differences between investing and

building is risk tolerance. Investors tend to have a more calculated approach to risk. They often rely on data and research to determine how much risk they are willing to take. In my early days, I jumped into investments without fully understanding the risks involved, which led to some tough lessons. I learned that being cautious and evaluating my risk profile is crucial for making smarter investment choices.

On the other hand, entrepreneurs often embrace risk as part of their journey. Building a business involves stepping into the unknown and taking chances on ideas that may or may not work. I remember launching a venture that I was passionate about, but it didn't succeed. That failure taught me that while risk is necessary, it's essential to have a plan and be prepared for setbacks.

Another key difference lies in exit strategies. Investors usually think about how and when they will sell their stake for a profit. They focus on maximizing returns, often planning their exit well in advance. In contrast, entrepreneurs may think about succession, aiming to build a business that can thrive even after they step away. My past failures helped me realize the importance of having a clear exit strategy, whether in investing or building. Understanding these differences has shaped my approach and made me more strategic in my business and investment decisions.

Time Horizons in Investment and Business

When it comes to investing and building a business,

understanding time horizons is essential. Investors often focus on short-term gains. They look for quick returns and want to see their money grow fast. In my earlier experiences, I made the mistake of prioritizing short-term profits. I rushed into investments that seemed promising but quickly fell apart. I learned the hard way that quick wins can sometimes lead to losses if you don't consider long-term potential.

On the other hand, building a business usually requires a long-term perspective. Entrepreneurs invest time, effort, and resources into creating something that can grow and sustain itself over many years. I remember when I started my first business. I wanted immediate success, but it took months of hard work to see any real results. It taught me the value of patience and perseverance.

Balancing these time horizons is crucial. While it's okay to seek quick wins in investments, it's essential to recognize that building a successful business often takes years. Long-term planning and a clear vision are vital for entrepreneurs. When I shifted my focus from short-term gains to long-term goals, I started to see real progress.

In the end, understanding the differences between short-term and long-term perspectives in investing and building can help you make better decisions. Learning from my past failures has shaped my approach, reminding me that true success often takes time.

Resource Allocation: Money vs. Time

In my journey as an entrepreneur, I've learned that

resource allocation is a crucial difference between investing and building a business. Investors primarily focus on capital—they want to put money into opportunities that promise a return. Early on, I often chased after quick investments, thinking that throwing money at a problem would solve it. However, I quickly realized that without the right strategy, my capital could vanish just as fast.

On the flip side, entrepreneurs invest a lot of time and effort into their ventures. When I started my first business, I poured countless hours into building it from the ground up. I learned that success doesn't just come from financial investment; it comes from dedication and hard work. While money can buy resources, time is something you can't get back.

I remember times when I underestimated the time needed for certain tasks, thinking I could just fund a solution. But those quick fixes often led to setbacks and additional costs. It taught me that true growth requires both time and money, but the time you invest is often what truly shapes the business.

In essence, while investors may focus on capital, entrepreneurs must balance their financial resources with the time and effort needed to create something meaningful. Learning from my past mistakes has shown me that successful building takes commitment and a deep understanding of how to allocate both money and time wisely.

Sustainability in Business and Investment

In my experience, sustainability has become a key focus in both business and investment. Early in my career, I overlooked the importance of sustainable practices, thinking they were just trends. However, after facing setbacks, I realized that building a business with sustainability in mind not only attracts customers but also creates long-term value. Customers today care about where their products come from and how they impact the environment.

When I shifted my focus to sustainable practices, I noticed a positive change. My business not only gained loyal customers but also operated more efficiently. For example, by reducing waste and using eco-friendly materials, I saved money in the long run.

Technology also plays a crucial role in both investing and building businesses. In my earlier ventures, I was slow to adopt new technologies, thinking they were unnecessary costs. But as I learned, technology can streamline operations, making processes faster and more effective. It also provides valuable data for making informed decisions.

Investors are now looking for companies that embrace technology and sustainability. They want to see businesses that are not only profitable but also responsible. In my journey, I learned that integrating these elements can transform a business. By focusing on sustainability and leveraging technology, I've turned previous failures into stepping stones for a brighter future, showing that thoughtful practices can lead to success in both business and investment.

Measuring Success

In my experience, measuring success in business and investment requires different metrics. For businesses, success often means growth, customer satisfaction, and profitability. I learned this the hard way; early on, I focused too much on short-term profits without considering customer relationships. Once I prioritized these aspects, my business flourished.

Investment success, on the other hand, is often measured by returns and market performance. I remember investing in a venture that seemed promising but didn't account for market conditions. When the economy changed, my returns plummeted. This taught me that understanding economic factors is crucial for both investors and business owners. While investors adjust strategies based on market trends, business owners need to adapt operations to maintain stability.

Ethics and responsibility are also essential in both worlds. I've faced situations where quick profits tempted me to compromise my values. Each time, I learned that sticking to ethical practices builds trust and long-term success.

Looking ahead, the future of business and investment is rapidly evolving. Trends like sustainability and technology integration are reshaping how we operate. I've seen businesses thrive by embracing these changes. My journey has shown me that whether you're building a business or investing, staying informed and adaptable is key. By learning from past failures, I now approach both worlds with a clearer understanding of what it takes to succeed.

Investing is the art of turning today's choices into tomorrow's treasures, crafting a legacy that goes beyond profit.

CHAPTER TEN

'THE POWER OF ASKING'

EMBRACE YOUR DESIRES WITHOUT HESITATION

The Art of Asking

Understanding the art of asking is a powerful tool in entrepreneurship. Many of us hesitate to voice our needs, often fearing judgment or rejection. However, asking for what you want can lead to unexpected opportunities and valuable insights. Throughout my journey, I've learned that the ability to articulate your needs clearly and persuasively can significantly impact your success.

In the past, whenever I faced challenges—be it business-related or personal—I often chose to handle them alone, avoiding involvement from others. This mindset only led to frustration and sometimes caused me to abandon my efforts instead of seeking solutions. I realized that isolating myself prevented me from accessing valuable perspectives and advice.

Now, I actively open up to trusted peers and mentors when I encounter obstacles. By sharing my challenges, I not only gain fresh insights but also benefit from their experience and expertise. Effective communication is key; being clear about what you need allows others to understand how they can help you. This collaborative approach not only fosters stronger relationships but also encourages a culture of support within your network.

In conclusion, embracing the power of asking can transform your approach to challenges. Don't shy away from seeking help; instead, view it as an opportunity for growth. By articulating your needs and opening up to others, you can navigate obstacles more effectively and enhance your entrepreneurial journey.

Overcoming Fear of Rejection

Overcoming the fear of rejection is a vital skill for any entrepreneur. Throughout my years of experience, I've learned that rejection doesn't define your worth; it's simply a part of the journey. While it can momentarily shake your confidence, viewing rejection as a learning opportunity can transform your perspective.

Rejection can sting, but it often provides valuable insights. Instead of allowing it to diminish your self-esteem, take a step back and analyze the situation. Ask yourself why it happened. Was your approach unclear? Did the timing feel off? Understanding these factors not only helps you grow but also equips you for future interactions.

Building confidence is essential when it comes to asking for what you want. Practice articulating your needs in various scenarios, whether in front of a mirror or with trusted friends. The more you practice, the more comfortable you'll become. Remember, even the most successful entrepreneurs face rejection; it's how they respond that sets them apart.

Handling rejection gracefully is equally important. Instead of reacting defensively, maintain professionalism and express gratitude for the opportunity to connect. This attitude not only preserves relationships but also demonstrates resilience and maturity.

In conclusion, rejection is not a reflection of your abilities but a stepping stone on your path to success. Embrace the lessons it offers, build your confidence, and learn to handle setbacks with grace. By doing so, you'll empower yourself to ask boldly and navigate the entrepreneurial landscape with resilience.

Identifying Your Desires

Identifying your desires is crucial for entrepreneurial success. Clarifying what you truly want in life can guide your decisions and set realistic expectations. One effective technique is to create a list of your goals, both short-term and long-term. This helps you visualize your aspirations and prioritize what truly matters to you. Reflect on your values and what satisfaction looks like in your ventures.

The science of asking reinforces the importance of making clear requests. Research shows that articulating your needs can significantly enhance your chances of achieving them. By asking questions and seeking advice, you gain valuable insights that can shape your decisions.

For example, I once ventured into a business expecting higher returns, only to find that the reality fell short. This experience taught me the importance of knowing what profit levels will satisfy me before diving in. It's essential to have a clear understanding of your financial goals and to ask others in the industry about their experiences.

Don't hesitate to reach out to mentors or peers who have navigated similar paths. Their insights can help you gauge the potential of a venture and ensure it aligns with your expectations.

In summary, take the time to identify your desires and be proactive in asking for information that can clarify your path. By combining self-reflection with effective communication, you'll be better equipped to make informed decisions that lead to fulfilling and profitable ventures.

The Psychology Behind Asking

Understanding the psychology behind asking reveals the mental barriers that often hold people back. Many individuals believe that asking questions makes them appear incompetent or uninformed. This misconception can prevent you from seeking the information you need to succeed. In reality, asking questions is a sign of curiosity and a desire to learn, not a reflection of weakness.

One effective strategy to overcome this barrier is to start by asking yourself questions. This self-reflection allows you to clarify your thoughts and identify what you genuinely need. By articulating your needs internally, you often refine your questions, making them more relevant and targeted. This clarity can lead to more meaningful inquiries when you engage with others, increasing the likelihood of receiving valuable answers.

Moreover, transforming relationships through asking can significantly enhance your connections with others. Open requests foster a culture of collaboration and trust. When you ask for help or insights, you demonstrate vulnerability, which can encourage others to share their knowledge and experiences. This exchange builds stronger bonds, creating a supportive network around you.

In summary, challenging the mental barriers associated with asking can empower you to seek the clarity you need. By first engaging in self-reflection and then making open requests, you not only gain valuable insights but also strengthen your relationships. Embracing the power of asking can transform both your personal growth and professional connections, paving the way for greater success in your entrepreneurial journey.

The Power of "No"

One essential aspect of the power of asking is understanding the significance of saying "no." While it may seem counterintuitive, rejection can often lead to new opportunities. In my experience, I've discovered that sometimes we become so focused on small gains that we overlook the potential for long-term profits. This short-sightedness can prevent us from pursuing ventures that truly align with our goals.

Learning to say "no" was a hard-earned lesson for me. Early in my entrepreneurial journey, I accepted numerous offers and opportunities that seemed appealing at the time. However, many of these choices ultimately distracted me from my primary objectives and diluted my efforts. After losing several promising prospects due to a lack of focus, I realized the importance of discerning which opportunities genuinely served my long-term vision.

Saying "no" allows you to redirect your energy toward ventures that align with your core values and aspirations. It's a powerful tool for prioritization, enabling you to concentrate on what matters most. Embracing this mindset fosters a sense of clarity and purpose, allowing you to cultivate more meaningful opportunities.

In conclusion, the power of asking encompasses not only the ability to seek out opportunities but also the wisdom to say "no" when necessary. By understanding that rejection can pave the way for greater possibilities, you empower yourself to make decisions that align with your long-term goals. This shift in perspective is essential for achieving sustainable success in your entrepreneurial journey.

Negotiation Skills for Success

Negotiation skills are vital for entrepreneurial success, and learning how to ask effectively can make all the difference. One of the best ways to develop these skills is to practice negotiating in everyday situations. Whether it's discussing a bill, haggling at a market, or even negotiating with family members over plans, these small interactions can build your confidence and refine your approach.

Start by identifying opportunities to negotiate in your daily life. Ask for a discount when shopping, request additional services without extra charges or simply express your opinions more assertively in discussions. Each successful negotiation reinforces your ability to articulate your needs and stand your ground. This practice not only hones your skills but also prepares you for more significant negotiations in business.

As you become more comfortable negotiating in casual settings, you'll find that your confidence grows. When the time comes to negotiate important business deals, you'll be better equipped to advocate for what you deserve. Remember, effective negotiation is not just about getting what you want; it's about creating win-win situations where both parties feel satisfied.

In conclusion, embrace the power of asking by actively practising your negotiation skills in everyday life. This approach will help you develop the confidence and techniques necessary to navigate larger business negotiations successfully. By making negotiation a regular part of your routine, you pave the way for achieving greater success in your entrepreneurial endeavours.

Asking in Professional Settings

In professional settings, the ability to ask for help can be transformative. Often, we overlook the expertise within our circles—colleagues, mentors, or industry professionals who could provide valuable insights when we're stuck. However, they cannot assist you if you don't ask. Embracing a mindset of asking is crucial for overcoming obstacles and unlocking potential solutions.

When making requests in the workplace, it's essential to approach the situation confidently and clearly. Start by identifying the specific help you need and whom to ask. Be direct yet respectful in your communication. A simple, "Can you share your insights on this project?" can open doors to invaluable advice. Practice this approach regularly to diminish any fear of rejection.

Moreover, overcoming the stigma associated with seeking assistance is vital. Many believe that asking for help signals weakness, but in reality, it demonstrates strength and a commitment to growth. Remember that collaboration often leads to innovation, and by asking for support, you encourage a culture of teamwork.

Real-life success stories abound of individuals who transformed their careers through the power of asking. From entrepreneurs seeking mentorship to professionals requesting feedback, these examples illustrate the profound impact of open communication.

In conclusion, embrace a mindset of continuous asking. It's not just about solving immediate challenges; it's about cultivating relationships and achieving lifelong goals. By asking effectively, you position yourself for growth, collaboration, and ultimately, success.

Ask boldly for what you want; your desires deserve to be heard. Embrace the power of your voice, and watch your dreams take flight.